SCRATCHES

AND

DEEPER WOUNDS

Rob Harle

ISBN: 978-81-19228-50-8

Cyberwit First Edition 2023
Rs. 200/-

Cyberwit.net
HIG 45 Kaushambi Kunj, Kalindipuram
Allahabad - 211011 (U.P.) India
http://www.cyberwit.net
Tel: +(91) 9415091004
E-mail: info@cyberwit.net

Printed at VCORRE PRESS.

Scratches and Deeper Wounds was first published in 1996 by Spinning Spider Publications PO Box 182 Nimbin 2480 Australia. ISBN: 0 646 29583 7

"...lost on a painted sky

where the clouds are hung

for the poet's eye

you may find me..."

(Jonathan Livingston Seagull)

Contents

"Puzzled" by Sandra Joran

Shooting The Breeze

Three weeks past the 'best by' date
dragged reluctantly, angrily
into existence with the force
of cold, old steel pliers
my characteristic, a furrowed frown
a frown on a new leaf of life.

Rising, falling, drifting with the breeze
resting now and then to hide
a city plot, the mountains green
the sea or coast, a place to dream
to reflect upon the absurdity of life
of birth and breath and death.

And now with good companion leaf
I've come to rest a while
in great long dead volcano's arms
whose primal landscape laughs too loud
whose village struggles under steamy skies.

The uniformed and drugged misfits
go floating onwards, past
and egos, grossly over size
strut the dirty street
stoned beyond courtesy's convention
with paranoia lines etched deeply
into empty faces, void.

And then pure love flows by

to set the paradox a-straight,
the valley mirrors cycles sure
of death and life and change
as living green disguises basalt bare.

Old clairvoyants waffle on
drowning in their flood of self deception,
and I wait for the breeze of synchronicity
weaving my philosophy of existence
upon my companion's loom
10,000 megabytes from Virtual Village.

Chthonian Vaults

Androgyny rises swollen and ripe
tempting, it caresses your mind easily
like the taste of melting chocolate,
a transformation of mental images
collected from past encounters
rounded, sensuous, piercing
gradually heat your inner core.
To become yin and yang
without sacrifice or scar,
to survive the boredom of mediocrity
you grow wings like Icarus,
only shrewd, you soar towards Pluto.
A journey of passion and provocation
to the deepest realms of nature's womb
where every move treads a razor's edge,
and blood and semen flow together
as archetypes yield their secrets.
Far from the purity of whiteness,
the glaring brightness of the Sun
you play in chthonian vaults of darkness,
moving forward with profane purpose
transcending synthetic moral pretence
the freedom you desire seems close.
Fly dangerously young hermaphrodite,
explore every chance with craving
swallow life with your voracious tongue
and consummate your destiny
in a ritual of solipsistic rapture.

Masks

This mask you wear today
cultivated
finely honed in light,
hours spent preening the reflection
mirror's lights
and mirror's gaze
to impress,
to bolster sagging confidence
dragged downwards slowly.
And yesterday's mask,
washed away
perhaps thrown in a corner
to decay like memories,
like childhood fantasies,
the puppets and the plays
have long since gathered dust.
What of tomorrow's mask?
Sleek, fashionable, fresh
projecting deep desires,
cool reflections
of grandiose games
or sighs of insecurity.
When your pantomime is played
and the final mask is made
What will be your next disguise?

Filtered Neon

Shadows merge then separate
dissolving in the warm night air,
the girls strut by,
proud flamingos with eyes electric
searching for signs in passing glances.

Glistening bodies, lovingly preened
move quickly through filtered neon,
high cut second skins of silk
shimmer, selling promises of pleasure
hard nipples threaten to burst
the delicate threads.

Hanging in the air,
the sweet fragrance of grass, floats
seducing the senses,
deals are negotiated
darkened doorways witness the transactions,
a frustrated business-man waits
lingering in the shifting shadows.

Erect veins ache with desire
as sharp cold steel ejaculates,
white death flashes
exploding into fiery flames,
supercharged flamingos strut out
ready for the second shift.

A priest strolls by immune and untempted
collecting used syringes from the gutter.

Glancing back and forth,
the business-man makes his play
her lips move slowly,
a note's exchanged; discreetly, quickly
caressing the fifty she forces a smile
her body seduces his eyes as he follows,
their forms merge in silent darkness
as the terrace hallway consumes them.
Outside in the gutter
a philosopher talks to passing shadows.

To Be Human

The mind deserts the body
as electronic components flash,
forcing flesh apart;
our primitiveness is challenged daily,
by an insidious digital invasion.
What is it to be human?
Merely a silhouette of love and hate?
A bag of disintegrating liquid stuff
held up by hollow bones?
When transgression of the heart means;
"Not enough memory - cannot execute".
Where social intercourse takes place
in cyberspace, syntactically
and body language is reduced to keystrokes.
The new masters, reign supreme
unaccountable to no one;
living in cyber-luxury in Silicon Valley
they define the circumference
the boundaries of our existence,
the edge of our `Virtual Reality'.
Addicted and dependant, hysterically
we scream for more and more,
possess me,
control my mind and soul.
Fear not the genetic engineering crew,
the multi-national directors,
the Church with story tellers old,
dictators and despots shrewd.
Fear the owner of the patents,
the owner of - The Chip.

This chip is God's new mask
enshrined in miniature,
with silicon pure and plentiful
the illusive , `Philosopher's Stone'.
What is it to be human?
A slave of every deception,
to every new `reality' proposed.
A primitive biological ectomorph,
walking upright,
endowed with self reflective core,
which shackles us to the delusion
of that self reflective core.

Plastic Cups

Beyond the morality of the righteous
time falls into frozen fragments,
stilted stills from the movie of life;
each actor outwardly secure
confident of their own truth,
inwardly, confused and cowering;
the catechism fails the holy.
Plastic cups roll aimlessly, irreverently
as the damp draft, drifts
chilling the soul's of searchers.
Confidence dissolves into frightened frames
as the cosmic joke permeates, slowly
peeling away the skins of security.
A young supple boy, plays
today an astronaut
flying past the moon to space.
A tired old man, dozes
embracing memories obsolete
flying past reality to resignation.
The mature man caught carelessly
oscillates with agitation
and flies nowhere, grounded.

The Ultimate Metaphor

The guardians haul on heavy doors
white Wellingtons, blood stained
give way to fashion footwear
the stench of terror, drifting
moves out across the sea
a caution to the whales
of mankind's wanton whims.

Today the product doesn't cower
nor freely ooze with blood
the blood is there though, only subtle
hidden, trapped in paint and canvas.
Paintings, sculptures, drawings
fade into carcasses before my eyes
the ultimate metaphor stuns me
like the art-speak stun-gun hype
stuns yuppies
mostly, sometimes vegetarian.

The obscenity of life and death
is celebrated in the House of Slaughter
offal transmutes to cheese and crackers
wine splashes like urine, cheaply
against the cool-room walls;
dressed to kill, many patrons
fat with credit, lean with taste,
whisper, as the trains thunder past.

Cyberspace encompasses you, assures you
it's all right,   it's all right
let yourself go, drift
slide into virtual.
Exploding through virtual into harsh
my soul regurgitates contamination
from lingering toxic visions
I run towards the cleansing sea
and realise far too late
meat = art = kill = cash.

Search For Reality

x
xag
xager
xagerate
all you can see
all your vital energy
every particle into mass
every vibrating wave into force
every chaotic dream into blood and dirt
and flesh
concentrate everything towards a centre
concentrate everything towards
concentrate everything
concentrate
concent
con
c

The Wall

"First, we'll take Manhattan,"
"Then we'll take Berlin."
Cohen's dream is flowering now
his army laying down its weapons,
Manhattan's not worth taking
and Berlin's great edifice,
though much too late,
has fallen, returned into dust.
Rising in its place, insidiously
a bitter, harder wall
impenetrable and thick,
pushing through the sky
to block the sun,
and cast its sombre shadow
over black and white and tan
with no respect for ancestral pleas
nor traditions strong and pure;
the charlatan in white, in Rome,
its architect and perpetrator.
A wall that separates
the good from God,
an eclipse of freedom's right,
this saint-maker, deceiver
myth monger in disguise
will be remembered long
with silent bitterness
by starving children's parents.
His henchmen stealing independence
from the congregation herd;

the 'fairy tale' disguised in purity
obscured by hypocrisy and fear
will be remembered long.
The perpetrator of misery,
puppet master of poor millions
deceives us to embrace our fate
and to live our only life,
a lie.

Reeboks and Dreadlocks

Byron Bay the sun's first sight
orange red shimmering strands
warm the cool blue sea
a promise of a bran-nu-day
it's just so good to be alive.

Holiday from gunmetal city smog
and stress levels way to high,
cholesterol blocks and traffic jams
cloud the price of Porsche's pride,
and the tension market hype
takes stock of gold commodities.

Room service, lovely morning smiles
Californian oranges squeezed just rite
a clutch of easy-over free-range eggs
brown shelled with buttered rye,
Dom Perignon to sparkle with the juice,
drink in the view from balcony on high.

Souvenirs for staff and friends
a bit of local craft, a pot perhaps,
a stroll around boutiques
and bistros clean and fresh
the streets all clean and washed
no dirt to stain the Reeboks, white.

Chez Jason for lunch I think
pate, Tasmanian Trout and Carlton Light.

No! I've got no spare change or love.
Call the police, the rangers brown
why not call the vigilante corp.
just move these filthy feral freaks
bludging 'round the bistros and the beach.

The Mayor's outraged his town's decay
crawling with life's vermin down
each lane and landscaped street
they shift in shadows cast
waiting in starvation, cold
to ask a stranger for a coin or crumb
foraging food from bins and gutters glint.

These bludging bastards, dirty hair
their rags a trademark of the poor,
shatter dreams of tidy towns
and every fantasy of middle class.
We'll drive them out with batten's thrust;
But where to hide the dreadlock gang?
Ship them out to an island bare
and make them build a colony there.
Call the police, the rangers brown
Why not call God to hunt them down.

Epitaph For A Car

I met a man who owned a car
an unhappy soul
tied down by bits of steel and glass,
I gave him my only pair of boots
and cautioned him to walk away.
I found them
cleaned and polished
in the backseat of his prison.
You fool
you fool I cried
and set his car on fire.
At last I knew he understood
as I watched him
walk towards the sunrise,
a smile upon his feet.

No Way Back

Sad neophyte philosopher
keen eyes below a crumpled brow
Observing houses all the same
in row on row brick on brick.
Mail boxes square on pipe
lined up like silent sentries
waiting for their orders.

Observing himself observing
by chance, a rare reflection
chills his blood and soul
an intruder in a foreign homeland
ancestral roots are severed
by a thought.

Quiet, quiet street
cemetery like in stillness,
houses as graves go line in line,
yellowing unloved shrubs
with sorrowed leaves
hang towards the dying grass
in quiet desperation.

A lonely cloud scuds mocking
across the void of blue
reflected in a sealed and screened
and curtained window,
protector of the uncremated dead
from nature's ardent love.

The philosopher has come too far
has seen and felt too much
What hateful God endowed him
with perception deep and clear?
What destitutions curse
has plagued this soul-less hell
where shadows come and go?

So where is left, the question begs
since purgatory has forced its hand
has shut its steely grated doors;
Ostracised by self so harshly
by careful observation the cord is cut
with no way back.

Towards A Centre

The probability of transparent thought
hurls itself against the wall of logic;
is our madness a cool facade
or the orange glow a foil
deeply lined in habit
but rising still.

Beyond the stage of perception
the dreamer becomes the dream,
moving forward in trance
signposts blur, fading
as consciousness adjusts its pitch.

Flowing, pushing toward an end
never veering from its centre
the circumference of knowledge
circles inwards, spiralling
as digital interactions define existence.

New travellers in cyberspace
hide, devoid of bodies
devoid of place, homeless
the concept becomes reality itself
and awareness contracts
into an endless binary loop.

Nothing Ever Changes

Block buster sell out, flashing lights
once in a lifetime chance, to dance
with Van Gogh and the crew from the Louvre.
Gallery A open each day,
Nine to five,
Come and see the Master's `in' pieces.

An hour in the queue your feet are hot,
but inside the colour fades that pain;
joyous now, you jostle and juggle
vying to view,
Sunflowers, Daffodils and Hay.

"Oh Look, that's worth ten million."
"Really. My dear, that's rather a lot."
"He does paint well though, I think."
"A little wild with coloured line!"
"Hem!"
"But still, the asylums look quite mad!"

The hype flows through and on;
fashion patrons hum and sigh;
twenty thousand tickets
trip the tarnished turnstiles
and another unknown artist dies.
"But I could have told you ......"

They're dying from starvation
from booting up with Ajax,

dying from disintegrating love
and from bullets bursting brains.
The unknown artist, alone and bleeding
cannot face Van Gogh
paralysed, in retrospect.

Had Things Been Different

Headlights glare then fade into coldness
a young man
no, Christ he's still a boy
shivers with emptiness,
alone and lonely
empty for a kindness to ease his pain.

His roof for the night,
a freeway overpass
stark lifeless concrete
grey,
curling tight in the corner
an embryo in the dirt
he aches for warmth
aches for someone to understand.

Sleep yields confused dreams
hell, heaven
he can't remember,
he grasps at the morning sun
feeling to thaw his frozen heart
the careless breeze
drifts the delicate rays away,
head down he walks hard
maybe someone in the city......

Below the mighty steel-grey bridge
a loving harbour glistens,
if only things had been different

broken family, booze - you know,
might of been on his way to university
medicine, science, the humanities,
he knew all about humanity.

The sun catches his eye as a tear falls
mesmerised he watches it fade below
falling, falling,
if only things had been different.
the harbour beckons
Come
Come to me.

A gentle pull sets him free
floating downwards
floating, floating,
he becomes an autumn leaf,
the harbour accepts him freely
no questions, no platitudes.

Workers trample for seats on their train
cars coalesce
forming another daily nightmare,
Executives
full of breakfast and self-importance
listen to the morning news.

Standing Straight

Swaying on the edge of hell,
again
the arrows fly, fast
the abyss looms overwhelming
deep purples change to charcoal black,
down, down.

Between the shadows concepts merge,
but danger hides in future's chance
and time is cheating life, insidiously,
like Dali's paranoiac-cannibalism,
the blackness devours my spark.

The cold hard steel of logic;
tungsten tipped with death,
drives the sliver of anguish
further than infinity,
and the ashes of hope drift away.

Gathering energy from emergency reserves
I climb towards the light
a glimmer in a distant nebula;
but then remember God is dead,
cruelly slayed by philosophy's elite.

I can't blame them in confession's cry.
they merely cleaned the slate
the slate of history, man-made grey
debased by religion's power and greed

and humans too afraid,
to take life standing straight.

Fragments

Ferns like filigree fountains
green beyond hue or tint
sway in silent softness
filling space in green on green
falling back beyond the greenness
to an endless vault
serene in tranquil contemplation.

Beyond the veils of consciousness
anticipating spikes of red
that threaten every stable state
the mind floats in apprehension,
the whirling starts a glow of red
building into thrusting red on red
the redness blazes into violent agitation.

Exhaustion overwhelms the fragmentation
as charcoal grey seeps in
surrounding life with mocking darkness
folding into deep blue midnight,
then mindless sleep in blackness
dispels the fear and anguish
of a life of shattered dreams.

The Second Coming

I look straight at eyes
that fall away nervously
only to glow later
in the brightness of rapture.

Kneeling before the computer altar
your mind churning through virtual
you understand at last,
God was the ultimate wound.

Smeared in violet across the lie of heaven
the obsessive programmer teases,
cajoles you to accept infinity
and the secrets beyond that invisible veil.

Still the pantomime of life plays on
Quantum, Chaos, Cyberspace
a jester in white Reeboks, casually
gave Schrödinger's cat its freedom.

The Zen buffoon has cracked the koan
but still the finger intimidates the moon.
The imposter entrenched in white in Rome
screams on, oblivious to the rising tide.

Your eyes now glowing, stand firm
as you announce the latest news:
the Messiah has come again
travelling in particle formation,

pulsing as waves, casually
along the digital highway
from infinity to absolute reality.

Logic's Thin Disguise

Professional exorcists grinning
sway to rhythms of primal harmonies
laughing loudly to discharge the tension
as the clouds cover the dangerous moon.
They recite the old magician's almanac
the rotting pages fall like shards,
as you listen to the sudden silence
you realise even choice is an illusion
draped in logic's thin disguise.

The shadows all wear lipstick
to hide their masks of pity
only powder white - you look like them,
and even though you hate them
they still control your mind.
Kneeling easily at the altar of ecstasy
bits of perfumed flesh and bone
penetrate the darkness of your tongue
as the world turns, your thoughts burn
and the slaves of passion perish.

You have paralysed yourself with beauty
thinking creation knows no end
but the lost artist runs naked
across the landscape of your soul
sketching you, that evil's night
is more desirable than virtue's day.
The canvas writhes with flying archetypes
as fate and free will crash,

only your tortured lips can save the world
so you discuss philosophy through the night
then read about your Daguerreotype of death
stained in black across the morning paper.

Mass Production

wandering through the canyons
of a high rise hell
with shadows cast, deep violet
changing into bruising black
the worth of mass production
agitated, teased my thoughts
then suddenly before me
icon like
a gnarled old tree stood proudly

alone

isolated in a field of tar
and concrete grey,
the answer hit me swiftly.

Doorways

Old doorways, silent sentinels
where the grey grit of a city
lies ensnared,
trapped in the folds
of peeling paint,
trapped in the scars
of shallow stone steps,
Old doorways dreaming
are overpowered,
consumed before their allotted span.

New doorways, gleaming glittering glass
are their successors,
where trendies gaze narcissistically
as they strut by,
where derelicts are confronted with faces
they cannot recognise,
where ladies of the night are embarrassed
to adjust their couture.

Romantic doorways, hide in fear,
desperate lovers seek them
after passion overflows,
teenagers seek them
after blue movies and strip shows,
winos' seek them
after, `time gentlemen time'.

Yesterday's newspapers

blown by a carefree city breeze
seeks them always.

Stones

The dream recurs
pushing the boundaries of tolerance
more persistent than stone,
stones that my chisel once gnawed
grain by grain
grit by grit.
The blood of the pen stains deeply
stones hard with age,
but dissolves away like clouds
or the morning mists,
yes, for me a steel scribed granite.
The hypnotic formulas dissipate
as the obsession keeps pushing,
forcing action,
I need songs and sins and sun
but more I need stones;
serene, strong and simple
to stand in defiance of mortality.

Betrayal

The baptismal fonts decay,
and information structures
breed like alien dictators;
fat rubber stamps rot slowly
as the assumption of integrity
collapses under hypocrisy's vengeance.
Force the young to live in gutters
squats and cardboard cut-outs,
build your National empires grand
which rest on stumps of misery;
your status rises, temporarily
with every option to oppress.
The young who only want a chance,
share the air and blood that's yours;
even more they trust you with their care.
Just like Judas you betray
not once, not twice,
but your enshrinement in the Chamber
perfects a continual betrayal
of lies and graft and horror.
Even as you drown your mind
and whisky spills across your soul,
you can't escape the burden of their hope.
Councillors of heavy hype and hail
empty, heartless, barren,
your life is a useless farce
if you sleep warm and weightless
when your children cower and freeze
in the sewer of your mind.

Homage To The Mud-Dauber Man

Through the filigree of space inspiration
comes in odd and other ways. Sometimes
we seek it in seclusion, sometimes it
comes by chance. It can rest for a
surface second, like Chuang Tzu's butter-
fly, or penetrate us deeply like the
sting of a wasp; indelible through time.
Too many years ago, surrounded by mud and
fragrant eucalypts, I met a mentor of a
man. He lit a blazing candle and I
perceived a world unknown. He loved all
frogs and was a man of Zen. The frog
chose my friend to use it as his symbol,
long before he ever heard of Zen. Totems
must choose their partners else they have
no fire or inspiration. His frogs are
full of life. They dive into inner space
defined by curve of clay or simply rest a
while upon the rim of pot and urn. With
smiles they watch their maker play with
dust and fire. We understand the way of
the potter-artist in watching silently
the wasp, though they remain the masters,
sure. My friend is a mud-dauber in disguise
guise with dexterity, intuition and the
single minded purpose of the little black
and orange dart. We shared the sun and
shadows and invented new realities until
the wine ran dry at midnight. But a

liaison of wasp and spider strains under
the threat of Damocles' sword. Now we've
gone our wandering ways, and he transforms the
the fire and earth and I the fire and air.

At The Roundabout

Sitting at the roundabout
my thoughts go `round and `round,
the ever watchful plastic horse
guards the saddlery door
and dreams of better days
when she was free to run;
her hound's-tooth blanket flaps,
tearing at the chill winter breeze.
Nearby an ageing painter dabs,
green and yellow ochre,
a new face for an old building.
A nun scurries into the watchmakers'
I wonder why she hurries
I ponder why she watches time,
perhaps her holy marriage
is marked in seconds,
her faith measured in hours or days.
The fragrance of warm bread,
rising from the hot bread shop
dances on the cool breeze.
Beside me the virtuosos, hopeful
swell the conservatorium walls,
they compete discordantly, obliviously
to the raucous traffic chorus.
An angel from hell, leathery
thunders by
his black chrome horse fuming, angry.
A mum with child encapsulated
pedals `round and `round

on an aged and rusting bicycle,
bits dangle from it
like the dangling thoughts, lost,
of the silent shoppers.
People stare at me,
suddenly their private thoughts
Stop!
What is he writing about?
Me?
I stare back blank-fully
then move my thoughts around
onto the roundabout
and go `round and `round.

The Man Who Would Be God
(A Genetic Engineer)

Hidden below the rim of perception
deep in the mire of madness,
the monster's mind moves fast
forcing manic myopic action;
his eyes spiral with fire,
burning,
heat, that only insanity can know;
his mission to map the human genotype
to store on-off on-off on-off
in a dark digital compression crèche,
the secrets of all life.
Like a pyramid he stands
aloof,
surrounded by a frozen desert
of apathy and ignorance.
He'll know from his dictionary of DNA,
his lexicon of life
the gene that makes us laugh,
the gene that makes us cry.
And when the mapping's done
Stage Two will start apace,
inter-uterine screening, screaming
in-vitro computer analysed fertilization.
Stage Three will enforce elimination,
he'll free the female body
from the barbarism of pregnancy,
then design and manufacture mutants,
clones and superhumans

in a loveless womb
of glass and stainless chrome.
No more nature's imperfection
Chance diversity, dissolves dangerously.
Control, control, control,
the suffering of humans abolished
sterilized from history.
Ectogenesis baby, that's the go.
No more suffering means no more sorrow,
means no more emotion
means no more wrenching of the heart
means no more compassion
means human = machine.

No Place For A Lady

There are secrets beyond her eyes,
deep secrets,
all eyes say something
but hers are strangely silent.
Stout and middle aged
the long black hair
bundled in a bird's nest bun
the lined and craggy face
betrays the silent eyes,
the cheap cotton dress
dirty, a tear across the hip
betrays a care-less person.
Brown hands, gnarled
the leather of too much sun,
the nails, short and jammed
with bits of grease and grit
pump petrol in the midday sun.
A hot wind stirs the oil-fuel fumes
as the bitumen garage stage shimmers,
no place for airs and graces
no place for a Lady,
this lady doesn't care.
Enigmatic stranger, distant
I can't read your eyes,
she doesn't care
perhaps her heart is free,
I can't tell.

City 5:00am

Eerily empty, the city at five am
a `still life' of despair,
the edge of a blue cold mirage
suspended, like purgatory
between false-dawn and dawn.
Greys change to black
then back to grey again,
pushed downwards by the damp draught,
drawn past drab facades
and steely mirror-black glass
reflecting itself reflecting itself,
in the sickly yellow lighting.

The scent of the underground
warm metallic, dusty
stale electric,
rises from the gutter grates
testing the memories of tramps,
those who rode the rail-road
in suits of silk
and careless confidence,
from warm home
to office obsession and back again,
and then - redundancy.

A faint hum, hum, hum
permeates the sacred silence
mysterious and alien
not wholly human,
not merely machine,

the ghost of the city moans,
a disembodied chant
surrounds the monuments,
marvels of human madness.
Silent street sweepers,
caretakers of this shadow world
sweep slowly, the sins
from last night's sacrifice,
sacrifices to love
to lust and longing.

Even the hard-core whores
desperate for a last trick,
leave this monstrous mausoleum
when the last neon flickers.
A black stiletto heal, scarred
wrenched free in hustle
in bondage in a footpath crevice
remains as testimony.
A siren far across the city
screams,
slashing the silence,
in a second all is dead again.

Frosted Fields

Walk the frosted fields today
now you are all alone,
the shadows of the ice
drip through the sky to you,
the grass beneath your feet accepts you now,
your life has nearly gone.
The world outside won't let you in,
you must pass from it
as it must pass from you;
your thoughts are lost in dreams of time
your voice is softer, quieter now
than when you were a fiery child;
your body's melting into frozen earth
your mind dissolving into darkened skies.

The Guillotine

Our global village waits
numb with disbelief
as the invisible decision rises
hovering high above humanity;
the particles of death honed
sharper than any rapier or razor.
The Rainbow sails as David,
across a dancing darting ocean
at peace with dawn and dolphin
to meet Goliath's genocidal guillotine.
Nurses, scientists, farmers chant
Chernobyl: Chernobyl: Chernobyl:
Vacant homes on abandoned farms
stare back at empty hospitals;
records, medical notes, paper bits
stained by blood red rain
lie in the strange ashen dust.
And our global village cries.
They speak in constructions of liberty
but the syntax is one of dire deception
their empty sentences
sentence every living organism
and echo across the sinking vortex
of an earlier Rainbow vision.
And we are silenced by superiority,
by the rhetoric of arrogance
and impenetrable imperialism.
And our global village screams,
Stop! Stop!

The guillotine has shuddered down
a hundred times or more,
down, down, down,
each descent disgorging
the inner hearth of Hades.
Evolution's history writhes
and the mutations wonder why,
at first the monstrous babies
with three hearts, no arms or eyes
are gently euthanized,
but the frequency of mutation grows
and our global village dies.

Lady In Black

She appeared from within the shadows
draped in darkness,
softly her black silk dress floated,
suspended
it revealed her thighs.
Eyes a-fire
piercing like a cat's
she scythed towards me;
my mouth moved but the words stopped,
almost imperceptibly
she smiled.
Closer
gracefully like a ballerina
she drew closer;
a shaft of light, shifting
seduced her slender neck.
She soared towards the light
her dress rising, spiralling,
slicing the warm night air.
My trembling hand reached out
further, further,
desperately I reached to grasp her arm,
as I closed my hand
she withdrew towards the shadows
and was gone.

Whore and Nun

the facade has split
is peeling
as the pupae eats your thoughts
cast from last years butterfly
has turned to evil's deeds.
hurtling through the tortured caverns
opening rigid darkened doors
'til exposed and naked
the final passion falls
and the moon casts splintered shadows
on the face of nun and whore.
"I'm not like that you rage,"
a hollow cry
for all to hear is false,
as whore and nun go dancing
down the highway of your psyche.
"Let's try this tango one more time"
where whore discards desire
where nun discards the habit
where both are mortal strangers
'til the lights go out at night.

Footprints

Scaling the crumbling cliff of destiny
I turn and let my eye fall
down down to the valley floor;
footprints disappear
filling with the dust of barrenness,
echoed unmistakenly
in shades of strictures far too harsh;
every advance eroded,
every move to imprint upon the path
a permanence,
is swept away unnoticed.

Reflecting, resting on a ledge,
the hardness of my granite loft
belies enduring limitations,
decaying basalt strewn across
a face of life intimidates mortality
and the fault line of life and death
narrows to a slit,
a fractured folding.

Higher now the valley fading
obscured by veils of mist;
temptation to dissolve into the misting
lessens with each weathered rock,
and mellowness betrays the ageing.

But all too soon I'll reach out gladly
to touch the rising moon.

Looking Towards Infinity

Draped in confusion I look towards infinity
listening I suffer the inevitability of isolation,
the whiteness of sacred flesh
mocks my feeble efforts
as the tired pages fall back to sleep.

Lost in the righteousness of abstraction
I charge mercilessly into the music,
the blackness of unanswered questions
mocks my feeble efforts
as the fools sing the Laws of Karma.

Drowned in the discord of smouldering wine
I court the winged messenger of fate,
the emptiness of unattended dreams
mocks my feeble efforts
as my mind drifts slowly away from its hinge.

And then a flash of hope ascends
I've foiled the arrows of the Philistines
the clarity of inspiration
mocks my feeble efforts
as I realise the answer lies beyond infinity
in a realm that few minds dare imagine.

Colours

Brown-red madder, madder
then
green, green, yellow green
yellow violet through
geranium lake and
carmine
black again,
grey
charcoal,
burnt to umber,
yellow
mars to violet
to violet
pale gold ochre stains
the prussian blue
cadmium scarlet screams
cadmium scarlet, cadmium scarlet
screams louder
scarlet vermillion, scarlet vermillion.
The orgy fades as
lemon yellow shifts to
chrome yellow now
cadmium orange drifts to
deep blood red
winsor red glows
alizarin crimson then
cobalt violet cools
magenta and prussian blue
indigo to cinnabar green

terre verte turns
intense cobalt green then
raw sienna and
burnt umber betrays
deep charcoal grey
lamp black fades to
ivory black then
blue black
into death.

A Poet's Place

those
days of wine and roses
are distant days indeed,
the wine's turned sour
the roses faded by pollution,
a poet's voice is [[[[[muted]]]]]
[[[[silenced]]]] by the turmoil
this terrifying technocracy
has cast him in a   void
the words just
fall

and

fall

upon a world that's numb,
a world that has abandoned him
and forced him down to die

alone.

Lost Café

Particles of melody drift easily
like veils of ash,
soft dust,
settling in napkin folds,
caught in timeless censure
where all things are possible.
Rhetoric raises ripples in the coffee
as cheeky sparrows swoop,
claiming the last crumbs of my daily bread.
The ripples surge to waves,
my cup jitters in its cradle,
debate, deliberation swerves,
swiftly from side to side.

Socrates' spirit stalks this café!
The thrust and parry
of well reasoned, well seasoned
reasons,
stick like frescoes
to the blazing black walls.

Sensuous aromas seductively tease
the drip, drip of black gold
pushes anticipation to a pitch
more searing than the search for truth.
I ponder how many philosophers
have caressed the rim with their lips,
suckled inspiration
from this porcelain chalice,

in blazing white.
Then drifting like the music,
static for an instant's pose
they dissolve into the street's reality,
their exit a frantic gesture
to reclaim a position in the world.

But they return, always,
older, battle weary
disorientated, demented
shunned by supermarket trolls
flogged by incessant neon whips,
raped by chrome and vinyl style.
Their minds dragged into bondage
at multinational fast-food chains
where coffee is served instant,
in an instant
with trans-Atlantic instant speak
and programmed instant smile,
where excellence means mediocrity.
Oh Socrates!
Was your hemlock draught in vain?

Sandstone To Ink

Of sandstone dust my spirit formed
a love of stone and water in
the dreaming of the Hawkesbury rift;
I dared to shape this nature's art
to carve and grind and penetrate
and share the vision of our primal source
to fire the soul's of others.

Inspired by sculptors past
Noguchi, Michelangelo and Moore
driven by a sacred muse
whose face remains illusive,
This spirit of the stone in silence
demands an awful price.

To dance on high with spirits fierce
is fraught with danger's sword,
Though double is the razor's edge
when dancing with the naked ape
whose tongue is sharply forked
and heart is hardened with desire
for more and more and more.

Art circus schooled in sabotage
adorned with superficial smiles
you couldn't violate my dream
nor change one mallet's thrust,
But coupled with these fragile bones
disintegrating far too soon

a transmutation of the means
has traded chisel in for sharper pen.
Now once more the ink will flow
or is it boiling blood
to trace its tracks across a page
instead of through the sandstone dust.

Scratches and Deeper Wounds

The hot bread shop breathes
warm fragrance of yeast and crust
awakening a primal urge,
a step or two
more temptations tease
coffee shop seduction
flat white, short black
cappuccino cream
the Choice is yours.
The balmy first flesh of spring
awakens other primal urges,
everywhere temptation
false hopes for new life,
temporary appeasement of deeper needs.
Stand clear, fuck, stand clear
four pall bearers frantic,
push past,
oblivious to piercing eyes,
oblivious to the stray dog
pissing on a post.
Her thin pale body,
lies motionless,
silent
flat upon the canvas stretcher,
O.D'd, indeed.
Is she breathing?
Yes, I think
hurry, hurry,
hospital seems so far,
her bearers,

barely friends
accomplices in street life hype
full of fear and flight and fight,
and hope; hurry.
Homeless, hopeless
street tough, street wise
some not wise enough to stay alive,
stand crying in the street.
The mourning penetrates their mask,
as secrets of their heart and care
flow down the gravel verge
and stain society's slate.
Her morning hit,
a simple scratch
has turned into a deeper wound.
As silent witness to this scene
of rage and life and love
I watched her die,
and wondered why

"Gigolette" by Sandra Joran

About the Author

(From first edition 1996)

Rob Harle was born in 1948, Sydney Australia.

He has training in Art, Architecture, Writing and Psychotherapy. Although he wrote consistently from 1978-96, his dominant mistress was sculpture. Marble, wood and sandstone works are held in various private and public collections.

A metamorphosis has been taking place over the years and the sculptor has returned to writer. Rob is currently studying Comparative Religion and Philosophy at Deakin University.

This is his first volume of poetry. Numerous poems and stories have previously been published in magazines, papers and journals..

Rob lives with his artist wife and geriatric cat on a rural property in the lush Nimbin Valley.

"My concern is to explore the phenomenon of consciousness and our `apparent' aloneness in the universe. Is life a literal or metaphoric illusion? Is reality, that frozen moment in the psychotherapeutic process of living where conscious and unconscious collide?"

Brief Biography (2023)

Robert Maddox-Harle (aka) Rob Harle now lives with his artist wife in Lismore, heart of the Rainbow Region. He is a poet, editor, artist and reviewer.

Writing work includes poetry, academic essays, and reviews of scholarly books, journals and papers. His work is published in journals, anthologies, online reviews, books and he has four volumes of his own poetry published – *Scratches & Deeper Wounds* (1996) and *Mechanisms of Desire* (2012). *Winds Of Infinity* (2016) and *The Blazing Furnace* (2022).

Recent poetry has been published in numerous anthologies and literary journals: Just a few examples -*Rupkatha Journal* (Kolkata); *Beyond The Rainbow* (Nimbin); *Poetic Connections Anthology*; *Indo-Australian Anthology of Contemporary Poetry*; *Rhyme With Reason Anthology*; *Asian Signature*; *Muse India*; *Voices Across The Ocean Anthology; Indo-Australian Anthology of Short Fiction. LIRJELL Journal; Homeward Bound Anthology; Voices Across Generations Anthology; World Poetry Yearbook; Temptations; Taj Mahal Review; Setu Magazine; Searching For The Sublime, Anthology.*

His past art practice for many years was sculpture, this was inspired by Zen Buddhism and Japanese aesthetics. Then after physical restrictions of health he commenced digital-computer art both for the web and print. His giclée images have been exhibited widely and featured both in, and as the covers, of various literary journals, academic textbooks and anthologies.

Formal studies include Comparative Religion, Philosophy, Literature and Psychotherapy - his thesis concerned Freud's notion of the subconscious and its relationship with Surrealist poetry.

Rob's main concern has been to explore and document the radical changes technology is bringing about. He coined the term *techno*Metamorphosis to describe this. This past concern is now moving towards helping to restore our abandoned metaphysical and spiritual modes of being through literature, especially poetry and digital art, with an emphasis on saving the natural environment.

He is currently a member of: *Leonardo Book Review Panel. (UK & USA);* Member of Editorial Board for: *Phenomenal Literature, (India); International Journal on Multicultural Literature (India); Ars Artium (India); Poetcrit (India). Ad Litteram* (India) and *Setu Magazine (USA)*
Full publications, reviews, selected writings and artwork are available from his website: https://www.maddoxharle.com

Other Books ... written, edited or co-edited by Robert Maddox-Harle (aka Rob Harle)

Alliances: *Three Lands Three Voices* (ed. Robert Maddox-Harle, Sunil Sharma, Jaydeep Sarangi), Authorspress, India. (2023)

Renew Relocate Restore (ed. Robert Maddox-Harle & Jaydeep Sarangi, Cyberwit, India. (2023)

The Blazing Furnace Poetry by Robert Maddox-Harle, Cyberwit, India. (2022)

Dancing the Light (ed. Robert Maddox-Harle & Jaydeep Sarangi, Cyberwit, India. (2020)

Winds of Infinity Poetry by Rob Harle Cyberwit, India. (2016)

Searching For The Sublime: Poems from Australia & India (ed. Jaydeep Sarangi & Rob Harle) Cyberwit, India. (2016)

Homeward Bound: Poems from Australia & India (ed. Jaydeep Sarangi & Rob Harle) Cyberwit, India. (2015)

The Land: Poems from Australia & India (ed. Jaydeep Sarangi & Rob Harle) Cyberwit, India. (2015)

PCK Prem Echoing Time and Civilisations (ed. Harle, Sharma & Sharma) Authorspress, India. (2015)

Indo-Australian Anthology of Short Fiction (ed. Harle, Sharma & Sharma) Authorspress, India. (2014)

Voices Across Generations: Poetry Past & Present (ed. Rob Harle) Authorspress, India. (2014)

Voices Across The Ocean: Poems from Australia & India (ed. Rob Harle & Jaydeep Sarangi) Cyberwit, India. (2014)

Indo-Australian Anthology of Contemporary Poetry (ed. Sharma, Harle & Sharma) Authorspress, India. (2013)

Building Bridges: Poems from Australia & India (ed. Rob Harle) Cyberwit, India. (2013)

Mechanisms Of Desire Poetry by Rob Harle Spinning Spider Publications, Australia. (2012)

The Clock by Diane Hosking (ed. Rob Harle) Spinning Spider Publications, Australia. (2004)

Scratches & Deeper Wounds Poetry by Rob Harle Spinning Spider Publications, Australia. (1996)

www.ingramcontent.com/pod-product-compliance
Lightning Source LLC
Chambersburg PA
CBHW022202160726
48282CB00024B/294
* 9 7 8 8 1 1 9 2 2 8 5 0 8 *